The Last Drop Of Rain

Reminiscing My Mother

Preeti Shamkule

BookLeaf Publishing

India | USA | UK

Made with ❤ on the BookLeaf Publishing Platform
www.bookleafpub.in
www.bookleafpub.com

Dedication

My Wonderful Readers......

This splendid compilation of Poetry is on grief, fade, aspiration, desire, ambition, despair, motivation and resilience.
It is dedicated to **You**...

You who are the **students** rumbling and tumbling in their life , who always have their spirits high.
You who are the **teachers** dedicated their life for the students.
You who are the **great women** standing as the pillar for the society and the world
You who are the **fathers** who struggle their existence in the family.
You who are my champions- **the teens**... the life of today's world.
You who are **the great lovers**, enjoy your life with ease.
You who are the **wonderful friends,** friendship speaks...
You who are the **artists, players and nature lovers..**
You who are my **Gyanis...,** the inseparable part of my life.
You who are my **beloved sons,** Neil and Aarav who brought me back from my death bed.

Preface

The Last Drop Of Rain is **very close to my heart.**

The very first poem is compared to my mother who was a rain in my life, she kept flourishing every aspect of my life and my meaning to be alive.

This is the compilation of poetry which acted as a support, mentor, guide to come out of my huge sorrow. I lost my beloved mother on 23rd November 2024, was completely shattered in her memories. Never imagined a world without her, coping up without her was a challenge. Handling all the relationships, sharing responsibilities, with a smile on face became near to impossible. Thus started putting my emotions on the paper which turned out into a wonderful poetry.

The Last Drop Of Rain is **a tribute to my mother Mrs. Rekha Gondode** who was my inspiration, my role model, my mentor, my guide.... I love you mom and will love you always forever and ever till eternity.

Acknowledgements

Gratitude is one of the strongest emotions.
It helps you to attract optimism in your life and
overcome all difficulties.
Law of Attraction plays a major role in an individual's
life.

I would like to express my sincere thanks to My amazing
dad (Mr. Gyandeo Gondode), My sweet brothers- (Dr.
Prakash Gondode ,Prem Gondode) , My wonderful son
(Neil Shamkule), My loving husband (Bhupendra
Shamkule).

They always helped me, guided me throughout the
process, Prakash was the first one to push and scold to
use my creativity to pen down into words, the most part
of the credit goes to him. I am really fortunate to have
these wonderful people around me.

Also a great thanks to Book Leaf Publishing House for
providing a great platform.

1. The Last Drop Of Rain

The land cracks, thirsty, bare,
A silence lingers in the air.
No rivers hum, no laughter rings,
No flowers bloom, no bird sings.

Once, the rain would dance and play,
Children ran in silver spray.
Paper boats sailed, winds would sigh,
Earth embraced the weeping sky.

But now, the final tear has bled,
The last drop falls—cold and dead.
Like a murder, cruel and slow,
Draining life with every woe.

Oh, mother, all is lost,
Dreams have dried, turned to dust.
Yet deep within, a whisper stays,
Hope will rise on brighter days.

One day, petals will unfold,
Rain will paint the earth in gold.
But your death, O lady fair,
Left a wound beyond repair.

Still, I wait through endless pain,
For healing touch of rain again.
The last drop of rain,
the last drop of rain.

2. An Unbreakable Bond

The house is quiet, your laughter gone,
Yet in my heart, your spirit lives on.
I remember the mischief, your cheeky grin,
The way you'd smile with a playful spin.

Your naughty ways, they brought such light,
You'd tease and laugh from morning to night.
No moment dull, with you around,
You filled our lives with joy unbound.

But it wasn't just fun you gave so free,
You were the lifeline, the heart of our family.
With wisdom and grace, you held us tight,
Guiding us through every wrong and right.

In your judiciousness, we found our way,
Through struggles, your strength would always stay.
The world may have lost you, but I see,
Your lessons and love live on in me.

Oh, how you cared, how you always knew,
What to say and what to do.
Your mischievous spark, your loving hand,
Together they built this family's stand.

Now that you're gone, I still feel your touch,
In every word, in every hunch.
I carry your naughtiness, your love, your grace,
In every step, I see your face.

You were the glue, the laughter, the guide,
Now in my heart, you'll always reside.
Thank you, Mama, for all you've done,
Your light lives on — you're never undone.

3. The Call That Heals

A phone rang out, so sudden, so clear,
His voice on the line, and she felt him near.
A simple sound, but it filled the space,
Turning her world to a different place.

Unaware of the storm she'd been through,
The loss of a mother, leaving her blue.
But his voice, so soft, so warm, so real,
Brought a comfort, a longing she could feel.

He didn't know the weight of her pain,
Yet his words seemed to wash her in rain.
She longed for his hug, to feel him close,
To cry on his chest, to let it all go.

Years had passed since they last spoke,
Yet this call revived a forgotten hope.
It took her back to a time so dear,
When love was young, and dreams were clear.

His dilemma, to come and hold her tight,
To comfort her through that endless night.
But fate had drawn their paths apart,
Yet he still carried her close in his heart.

He blamed the world, the cruelty he saw,
As she lived in another, and he in his law.
But yearning for her was his constant fight,
A longing deep, hidden from sight.

She in another family, him in his,
But their hearts still whispered the same bliss.
He knew, in that moment, only he could understand,
The depth of her sorrow, the ache in her hand.

Her loss was great, but his call so kind,
Took her to places where peace she could find.
Though they couldn't be, though worlds had changed,
In that phone call, their souls still arranged.

The world may be cruel, yet here they are,
Connected by distance, no matter how far.
A special call, so full of grace,
A brief moment where they both found their place.

4. Tired Of The Blame

I am the mother, the wife, the guide,
The one who stands with arms open wide.
Yet every day, it's the same old song,
I carry the weight, though something feels wrong.

I wake before dawn, I toil through the night,
Forgetting myself in the blur of the fight.
I give all I have, with no end in sight,
But where is the thanks, the love, the light?

My hands are worn, my heart is frayed,
Yet I am the one who must always trade.
Trade my dreams for theirs, my peace for their need,
A life of devotion, but where do I feed?

I've given my all, my body, my soul,
But the gratitude's gone, and the cracks take their toll.
I am not just a title, a name to be called,
I am a woman, with hopes, who feels small.

I want my time, my space, my voice,
To be seen for who I am, not just by choice.
To have a moment to breathe, to stand on my own,
To be respected, not just overthrown.

For all that I've given, for all that I've done,
I long for a day where I'm seen as someone.
Not just a mother, not just a wife,
But a lady who deserves her own life.

I'm tired of the blame, the endless demand,
I long for a moment to take a stand.
To say "I am worthy," to hear "I see,"
A world where my worth is more than just me.

5. The Gem's Heartache

She worked through nights, her soul alight,
A girl who toiled, with all her might.
She shaped his words, his confidence grew,
Taught him to speak, to stand, to pursue.

With patience and love, she built his name,
Through sleepless hours, without any fame.
She molded him, with every care,
A gem of a teacher, rare and fair.

In return, a title, a word so sweet,
"Gem" he called her, for all she'd complete.
Her heart danced, for a place was made,
In his life, where trust and respect stayed.

But fame bloomed, and with it, pride,
He climbed high, forgetting her side.
Once a bond so pure, now torn apart,
Her love for him still filled her heart.

Blame was placed, with a flick of a hand,
A small mistake, and they couldn't withstand.
The irony deep, as she watched him rise,
His arrogance clear in his once-soft eyes.

She longed for the purity, the serene grace,
Of days long gone, in a familiar place.
Now adrift in a sea of confusion and doubt,
She seeks the connection that was once so stout.

But time has changed, and so has he,
Lost in his world, blind to the plea.
Her love remains, unwavering, true,
But the bond they shared is now askew.

She dreams of a time when they'd reunite,
To reclaim the glow of that gentle light.
Yet here she stands, in silence and grace,
Longing for the purity, for that lost embrace.

6. A Silent Cry On Your Birthday

Today, my love, the world should sing,
For it is your day, the joy you bring.
But here I stand, in shadows deep,
Fighting to keep our hearts from sleep.

My mother's gone, the pain so raw,
A loss that shakes me to my core.
In this silence, where tears hide,
I seek your arms, to stand beside.

I know I've faltered, and I've cried,
But love still burns with the hope inside.
Yet you, my love, turn from my plea,
And leave me stranded, lost at sea.

I wanted to celebrate, to make you smile,
To hold you close, if just for a while.
But the distance grows, unspoken, wide,
A silent gulf between us, where love once tried.

I know you're hurting, I feel it too,
But love, my dear, what will we do?
If we can't speak, if we can't see,
What's left of us, if not you and me?

So, on your birthday, I make this plea,
Come back to me, don't let this be.
For I am here, though torn and frail,
I need your love to help me sail.

Through grief and silence, I still yearn,
For the man I love, for your return.
Though words are few, my heart is loud—
In love, in loss, forever proud.

7. Nostalgia: A Girl's Reflection

In a small town where the winds would sigh,
A little girl played beneath the vast sky.
With a big, fat family, laughter would roam,
A house full of love, yet struggles to comb.

Her mother, the pillar, stood strong through the years,
Wiping away sorrow, calming all fears.
Five hearts, each different, but brilliant in might,
In the glow of their talents, they'd shine so bright.

One excelled in books, so sharp and so wise,
Another painted wonders beneath moonlit skies.
A writer, a poet, with words as her art,
A leader whose vision set her apart.

Through struggles, they helped, side by side,
With each little triumph, they'd laugh, they'd confide.
Playing with friends, the world seemed so wide,

But fate had a plan, to guide her with pride.

One day a prince came, with promises grand,
And swept her away to a faraway land.
The kids, they grew up, their paths now clear,
Doctors, engineers, all with a bright career.

But the heart still remembers those simpler days,
Of family, of struggles, of childhood's maze.
And though they are grown, the bond will never end,
For those roots in the town, are where dreams began to
blend.

46. Desires Of The Heart

She dreams of days where laughter's free,
A life with him, as bright as the sea.
Where love flows soft and dreams entwine,
Her heart beats steady, knowing he's mine.

She longs for someone who'll truly see,
The quiet pains, the thoughts that flee.
To understand the depths of her soul,
To make her feel heard, to make her whole.

In moments dark, when skies turn gray,
She wishes for her mother's gentle sway.
A hand to hold, a soft embrace,
To lift her spirits, to light her face.

A home of warmth, where love will stay,
With two small children, laughter at play.
A family strong, united in cheer,
A life of joy, with none to fear.

Her desires simple, yet so profound,
A love that's patient, a life unbound.
For happiness, for peace, for grace,
In each moment, she'll find her place.

She dreams of joy, pure and bright,
A heart at peace,a soul alight.
She longs for laughter, soft and true,
A life where all her hopes come through.

In quiet moments, her heart takes flight,
Seeking happiness, in day and night.

9. Unwavering Blessings

I know you, my son, from the very start,
A wonder, a spark, you've captured my heart.
Since childhood, you've always been true,
A unique soul, with dreams to pursue.

I've watched you grow, and I see it clear,
The path you'll walk, without any fear.
In your designing world, they'll praise your name,
For your brilliance, your vision, your rise to fame.

You'll lead the way, a top designer, so grand,
Crafting masterpieces, with your steady hand.
A future of wealth, and success so bright,
You'll shine like a star, lighting the night.

With name and fame, and riches untold,
You'll stand on the podium, fearless and bold.
Business tycoon, with power and grace,
The world will salute you, in every place.

Your strength, your wisdom, they'll all see,
For you are destined for greatness, my dear, and I
believe.
Your grandma and I will be proud of you,
As you conquer the world and make dreams come true.

Remember, my son, as you rise so high,
You carry my love, you touch the sky.
No matter the heights that you will attain,
You'll always be mine, through joy and through pain.

10. A Spark Unseen

In the quiet of mornings, I rise with grace,
A teacher, a dreamer, with passion to chase.
I stand in classrooms, with hearts to ignite,
But still, at home, I feel out of sight.

You speak of success, of wealth, and of fame,
But I carry a fire that burns with no name.
You've built your empire, with suits and with ties,
Yet I build futures, where true power lies.

You see me as just the wife, the guide,
But I am more, I've nothing to hide.
I'm not defined by your world of suits,
I've my own roots, my own pursuit.

I've worth beyond what you'll ever see,
A spark that longs to set me free.
In every lesson, in every word,
I shape the future, I'm heard and stirred.

I'll rise, my love, though you may not know,
I'm not the shadow, I'm the light that glows.
I'll prove my place, in the world so wide,
No longer silenced, no longer denied.

I'm not just a wife, I'm a force, a flame,
A teacher with dreams, an untamed name.
I'll show you, my love, what I am worth,
And prove my spark in this world's rebirth.

11. A Promise To Her Dreams

With every breath, with every beat,
I promise you, Mom, I won't retreat.
Your dreams for me, so pure, so bright,
I'll carry them with all my might.

You dreamed of seeing me reach the stars,
To rise above, no matter how far.
To see me stand where legends are made,
In the light of success, unafraid.

I swear to you, with all my soul,
I'll chase those dreams, I'll make them whole.
For you, I'll rise, I'll break the chain,
Turn every hardship into gain.

You wished for wealth, for fame, for name,
For me to stand in the hall of flame.
I'll build that legacy, brick by brick,
Climbing mountains, fast and quick.

To see your pride in my success,
I'll reach new heights, I'll do my best.
Every wish you held in your heart,
I promise you, I'll play my part.

In your dreams, I'll find my way,
To live the life you've wished each day.
For you, dear mother, I will become,
A story of triumph, second to none.

12. Radiance

Today, we celebrate the spark in your eyes,
The endless questions, the dreams that rise.
Adolescence, a journey both wild and free,
Where every step holds a new discovery.

You are not just learners in these halls,
But dreamers, explorers, who answer the calls
Of curiosity, fun, and growing pains,
Chasing knowledge through sunshine and rains.

In your laughter, I see the world unfold,
A tapestry woven with stories untold.
You're the future, with hearts full of grace,
With every mistake, you'll find your place.

Though the path may sometimes seem unclear,
Remember, you're never alone, never in fear.
Together we'll learn, we'll stumble, we'll rise,
With courage and kindness, let's reach for the skies.

So on this Children's Day, I say to you all,
Embrace every moment, stand proud, stand tall.
For the world is your canvas, so bright, so wide,
And with each step you take, let your true self collide.

May your journey be filled with joy, with fun,
As you chase the stars and soak up the sun.
I'm here as your guide, your teacher, your friend—
And I'll walk beside you, right to the end.

13. The Lovers Who Never Met

In the moonlit pages of a distant tale,
Where Laila and Majnu's hearts set sail,
Through deserts wide and heavens high,
They called each other beneath the sky.

Heer and Ranjha, with love so pure,
Met by fate, yet found no cure.
Their souls entwined, but bodies apart,
Two yearning echoes from a single heart.

Soni and Mahiwal, side by side,
Their love a river, wild with tide.
Yet the shores were cruel, the path too steep,
And dreams of reunion lost in deep sleep.

Romeo and Juliet, in Verona's night,
Spoke of love with a fire so bright.
But fate's cruel hand stole the final kiss,
Leaving behind a world in abyss.

We remember them still, these lovers so true,
Their stories etched in the skies so blue.
But I must ask, with a longing deep,
Could they not have woken from love's cruel sleep?

Why must the heart break before it's whole?
Why must the stars dim their guiding role?
Could not their love, so endless, soar,
In a world where distance is no more?

Ah, poets of old, do you not see?
Love need not end in tragedy.
A happy ending, free from pain,
Could still immortalize love's reign.

For in every tear that falls for the past,
A hope remains — that love will last,
Not in sorrow, but in joy complete,
Where lovers meet, and hearts find peace.

14. A Heartfelt Ode

Oh, My Gyanis my Class X, my clever crew,
With laughter bright and hearts so true,
You've made this year a memory sweet,
With pranks, and mischief, and schoolyard feats.

The lunch break came, and there you'd be,
Snatching tiffins so sneakily!
Teasing friends with playful jest,
Your joy and fun, you shared your best.

Skipping lectures, yet still you shone,
On the grounds, together, you've grown.
Troubling teachers with your charm,
But in your hearts, you meant no harm.

You're a masterpiece, this I know,
The mischief, the smiles, all set aglow.
But on the day of farewell, my dear,
As I was at the dispersal
You forgot to click that photo near.

But you, my students, are my treasure,
Beyond any picture, beyond any measure.
Though today is special, so are you,
In every way, both bright and true.

Now the time has come, the boards await,
Be serious, focus, it's not too late.
Trust yourselves, give all you can,
For I believe in each of you, every man and woman.

Top the school, make your name shine bright,
On the board, let your success take flight.
Don't feel pressure, just do your best,
Give 100%, and forget the rest.

You can do it, I know you will,
Your dreams are close, they're yours to fill.
So rise to the challenge, with all your might,
I'm so proud of you—keep reaching the height.

15. Forever Home In My Heart

The world feels quiet, still, and cold,
Since you've left, a heart turned old.
I stand alone where you once stood,
Wishing I could turn back, if I could.

The whispers of your gentle voice,
Now a memory, a fleeting choice.
Your warmth, your love, your soft embrace,
Now vanish like the fading trace.

I search for you in every room,
In the sunlight, in the gloom.
Your smile still lingers in my mind,
A precious gift I cannot find.

Yet in my heart, you're not gone,
Your love still plays, a quiet song.
You taught me how to face the storm,
And how to love, and how to mourn.

Though the earth has claimed your rest,
In me, you live — you were the best.
And as I walk this life alone,
I carry you, forever home.

16. The Artist I Met

I met an artist, with colors in his mind,
A spark in his eyes, a heart so kind.
With every brushstroke, he painted the skies,
Transforming the world through different eyes.

His humor was light, his spirit so free,
He found beauty where others couldn't see.
With laughter and joy, he turned every day,
Into a masterpiece in his own unique way.

His approach was different, a twist, a turn,
In every moment, there was something to learn.
He made life vibrant, with shades bold and bright,
Where shadows faded, replaced by light.

He taught me to smile when the world feels gray,
To find the magic in the mundane, every day.
Through his art, he showed me the truth—
That life's most beautiful when we embrace our youth.

I met an artist, and with him, I found,
A world of wonders, unbound, unbound.
Through his lens, I saw life anew,
A canvas of dreams, painted in every hue.

17. The Fire Within

In shadows deep, I stood confined,
A whispered dream, a tethered mind.
A silent voice, a stifled art,
A canvas blank, a caged heart.

But then you came—a force, a fire,
A call to rise, to reach, aspire.
"You are not dust, nor fleeting shade,
You are the storm, the light, the blade."

No longer lost in fear's embrace,
I carved my name, I found my place.
Words once hushed now boldly soar,
A poet's soul can hide no more.

A legacy in ink shall stay,
A spark to set the world ablaze.
No longer bound, no longer still—
I shape my fate, I bend my will.

Through trials forged, my spirit rose,
A symphony where silence froze.
Each wound became a mark of might,
A beacon set to pierce the night.

No chains remain, no echoes fade,
I stand unbowed, no more afraid.
The past may whisper, doubt may call,
Yet I shall rise—and never fall.

For history waits on none but those
Who dare to bloom, who dare to glow.

18. A Voyage Of Dreams And Memories

The sun once bathed in golden light,
With laughter ringing, hearts so bright.
A festival of hues, a dance so free,
With friends and love—a jubilee.

The air was rich with spice and cheer,
Mouths rejoiced in feasts so dear.
Music soared, and feet took flight,
Till dusk embraced the fading light.

Yet when the colors bled to night,
A hush of sorrow dimmed the sight.
For soon, the time would slip away,
And dawn would steal a friend to stay.

Our voices clashed, our tempers high,
The twenty-sixth jan, beneath the sky.
A word too sharp, a wound too deep,
Left guilt within, too strong to keep.

But then, my friend, with whom but you?
Who else to argue, bold and true?
Your taunts, your jests, the fiery spree,
Will echo now in memory.

A heart once bold, now weighed with woe,
For distant lands he must now go.
Though oceans called, he'd soared before,
This time, the ache cut to the core.

For in his home, his soul was bound,
Wife's love that bloomed in sacred ground.
A mother's warmth, his children's glee,
Now memories across the sea.

No words could frame the pain we knew,
No farewell spoke the love so true.
Yet eyes that gleamed with silent grace,
Held all the prayers time can't erase.

So go, my friend, let dreams ignite,
Let stars above still guide your flight.
May fate embrace you, strong and wise,
With joy that never bids goodbyes.

19. A Mother's Vision

In the face of storms, in trials so deep,
You held a vision, your promises to keep.
Through struggles and hardships, you never did sway,
Your eyes on our future, you paved the way.

With every challenge, you stood so tall,
A beacon of strength, you answered the call.
For us, you dreamed, with love as your guide,
A vision of success, where hope could reside.

In every field, you found your grace,
In every charm, you left a trace.
Your heart knew no limits, your will knew no end,
A mother, a mentor, a constant friend.

Your never-give-up spirit, so fierce and true,
Has shaped us, inspired us, in all that we do.
You taught us to rise, to chase and to climb,
With faith in our hearts, you made our dreams shine.

For in your vision, we find our own,
A legacy built on seeds you've sown.
I'm proud of the strength you always show—
A mother's love, the purest glow.

20. Unheard Cries

Why honor her for just a day,
when respect should live in all you do?
Empty words are not the way,
let actions prove your love is true.

You raise your voice but never hear,
the silent pain within her chest.
Demanding respect through guilt and fear,
yet failing to give her your best.

When did you last take time to see,
the world through your own children's eyes?
Did you guide them patiently,
or drown their voice in angry cries?

One stands lost in shifting tides,
his heart unsure, his mind confused.
He longs for you to stand beside,
not scorn him when he's bruised.

The other one looks up to you,
his hero, strong and wise and bold.
But what he learns from what you do,
is more than all the tales he's told.

And she, the woman by your side,
with gifts the world can plainly see,
yet in your words, her hopes collide,
drowned beneath your apathy.

Be more than words upon a screen,
let love be seen in what you give.
Respect is real, not just a scene,
but woven in the way you live.

21. Gentle Echoes In The Storm

In twilight's gentle, weary glow,
A father's heart bears silent strife;
Through burdens that no words can show,
He weaves his love through thorny life.

In roles of husband, son, and friend,
The world demands a flawless frame;
Yet deep inside, old wounds may mend,
While judgment burns with ruthless flame.

He labors on as bread and shield,
A mentor whose love lights the way;
Though storms of anger may sometimes yield,
He stands resolute come what may.

Conflicts arise with those held dear,
When words like arrows break the peace;
Yet hidden behind each falling tear,
Lies longing for a sweet release.

In moments dark, his spirit weeps,
Yet quiet strength endures the pain;
For in his heart a promise keeps,
That love will rise like gentle rain.

He sees the clash of differing views,
A family split by silent pain;
Yet still his love, like morning dews,
Will bring them hope to rise again.

A vow is made to calm the storm,
To temper wrath with gentle art;
Transforming strife to acts of warm
Care that heals each wounded heart.

Now in the glow of hope reborn,
Each smile reflects a tender start;
A promise to embrace each morn,
With love that mends the fragile heart.

22. I Understand

In the quiet hours I sense your pain,
A burden carried deep inside,
You bear the weight of love and strain,
While harsh demands refuse to hide.

A silent hero, true and strong,
A father, son, and loving guide,
In every role you strive so long,
Though doubts and trials often collide.

You try to paint each day with cheer,
Yet shadows fall where light should gleam,
Your earnest efforts disappear,
As fate disrupts your hopeful dream.

I listen when your silence speaks,
In whispered sighs your heart confides,
Though words elude the truth you seek,
I hold your soul where love abides.

When clash of views with son ensues,
A fiery duel of pride and claim,
I see the strain that you peruse,
And feel the weight of every blame.

When bitter rains of fault descend,
And respect seems lost in endless night,
Your weary spirit yearns to mend,
Yet finds a spark of hope so bright.

As breadwinner, you shoulder more,
Fulfilling every need and plea,
The heavy load you must endure,
Testifies to your loyalty.

Beloved, know this journey's shared,
Our lives entwined by fate's design,
Though burdens leave our hearts bared,
Together, love will redefine.

Step gently into others' shoes,
Embrace the views that calmly flow,
Within each heart, a tale accrues,
And empathy begins to grow.

You'll shine as husband, father, son,
A guiding star through every test,

In trials, your strength is never done,
For in your love, we are all blessed.

45

Adapt to times with open heart,
Though changing minds may test your might,
Let wisdom be your compass chart,
To merge the old with fresh insight.

I know you'll rise above the storm,
My darling, cherished, ever true;
In every role, you'll transform,
These words of love I speak for you.

23. Ethereal -Echoes of Laughter Unseen

Laughter wove through twilight's hue,
A golden dusk, a bond so true.
Carefree steps and voices bright,
A day of joy, purest light.

But fate, a thief, unseen, unheard,
Struck the air with a shattering word.
A father lost, a soul untied,
His spirit soared, the earth had cried.

My lips, a gate to grief untamed,
Held a truth both raw and maimed.
How does one break a heart so whole?
How do you darken a shining soul?

He stood, unknowing, lost in time,
Before the chime of sorrow's rhyme.
Yet as the weight of truth unfurled,
His laughter stilled, his world unwhirled.

Night grew thick with haunted air,
As silence whispered soft despair.
I walked alone, the shadows deep,
Aching cold that none could keep.

The bridge, a passage steeped in woe,
Where spirits tread with steps so slow.
The tea shop, shuttered, dark, and bare,
A void where warmth once lingered there.

Fear curled tight around my chest,
Each breath a ghost, an icy guest.
School stood veiled in eerie shade,
A prank of darkness, coldly played.

Yet dawn arrived, as dawn must do,
To chase the night with golden hue.
Fear dissolved in light's embrace,
A lesson carved in time and space.

Life will dance and death will call,
Both are threads—a fate for all.
Yet courage walks where shadows creep,
And truth will wake where sorrows sleep.

24. A drift in the Tempest of Longing

Upon these waves, fierce and wild,
I sail alone—storm-tossed, exiled.
No steady hand to still my fears,
No whispered hush to calm my tears.

His touch—once solace, soft and true,
A tether strong, a golden hue.
He read my silence, felt my ache,
Held my sorrow for my sake.

A glance—no words, yet he would know,
Like moonlit tides that ebb and flow.
Respect adorned his every phrase,
Love shone through his steady gaze.

Now, the gales of fate conspire,
My soul—a vessel lost, entire.
I seek his warmth, his voice, his light,
A beacon in this endless night.

Oh, cruel world, with jagged teeth,
Spare me grief, grant me reprieve.
Let him return, let him be near,
To quell the storm, to still my fear.

And so, with eyes that do not wane,
I wait beneath the sky's refrain.
For love that mends, for hands that hold,
For him—to come, to make me whole.

25. Silhouettes Of Fear

She walks alone beneath neon's glow,
A silent prayer in footsteps slow.
The city hums, indifferent, cold,
Yet shadows lurk in stories untold.

A girl of twelve, her laughter bright,
Now silenced by a thief of light.
Who gave you the right to shatter her soul,
To tarnish innocence, to leave a hole?

She is not a whisper, not a prey,
Not a pawn in the games you play.
Her worth is not for hands to take,
Nor for a world to bend and break.

Equality—does it truly breathe,
Or just a promise, meant to deceive?
Still, she shudders in taxis late,
Still, she fears the hands of fate.

A trusted face, a brother's guise,
A lurking dread in friendly eyes.
Does blood not boil? Do hearts not ache?
When dignity crumbles, when souls forsake?

Dear men, I plead—unshackle the chains,
Erase the scars, unwrite the pains.
See in her, the mother who gave you breath,
The sister who shields, the love that's left.

Not a whisper, not a prey,
Not a toy to toss away.
Raise your hands not in disgrace,
But in honor—let respect take place.

For when fear dies and justice wakes,
The world will heal, no heart will break.

26. Resurgence

Through labyrinthine paths of endless night,
Where echoes wail and hopes take flight,
A tempest roars, a ruthless tide,
Yet deep within, the flames abide.

As infancy fades, the trials unfold,
A timid soul, yet dreams untold.
Faltering steps, yet forward bound,
In stardust dreams, new worlds are found.

The teenage tempest, fierce and wild,
A fractured heart, a restless child.
Amidst the storm of doubts that rise,
A phoenix stirs behind the eyes.

Then comes the weight, the adult war,
A battlefield with unseen scars.
Aching shoulders, weary bones,
Yet strength is carved in molten tones.

The world shall judge, the tongues shall burn,
Yet diamonds form when pressures churn.
Not all that glitters fades away,
But gleams in light, come break of day.

So rise, O soul, from ash and mire,
A golden blaze, a burning pyre.
Through every twist, through every bend,
Your spirit soars, it shall transcend.

27. Treasure

He stumbled upon a secret chest,
A trove of poems, her heart confessed.
Each line a whisper, each word a dream,
Her collection, like stars, a shimmering beam.

He read them all, one by one,
Feeling the pain, the joy, the sun.
With every verse, he saw her soul,
A world of emotions, making him whole.

He asked her, "May I keep just two,
The ones that touched me, that felt so true?"
But with a sigh, she shook her head,
"No, my dear, these words are my thread."

"These poems are my treasure, my life's song,
They've carried me when the road was long.
They are my truth, my masterpiece,
My memories, my pain, my peace."

So he let them go, her treasures untold,
For he understood her world, so bold.
He may have found her poetry's grace,
But the real treasure was her embrace.

28. The Serene Haven

In days of yore, when years did flee,
I wandered far, o'er land and sea,
Till I didst come, with heart astir,
To a place where time didst gently blur.

The trees, they whispered in soft repose,
Greenery's bloom in endless rows,
And flowers, as though from dreams did spring,
With petals kissed by morning's wing.

I walked the path, my feet did tread,
But lo, I stopped, my heart was led,
To the beauty, pure, that met mine eyes,
The peaceful wind, the softening skies.

The sun, it rose upon the lake,
A golden hue, the dawn did break,
And birds did sing, their melodies sweet,
As if the world itself did greet.

I thought of days in granny's glade,
Of forests deep and fields we'd laid,
Of summers spent in nature's arms,
Untroubled by the world's alarms.

Now here, I stood, in quiet bliss,
Embraced by peace, by nature's kiss.
A tranquil balm, to soothe the soul,
A perfect moment in nature's role.

29. A Journey of Time

In the second year, on a quiet day,
A boy met a girl in a familiar way.
Her smile, like sunshine after rain,
But this wasn't the first time they'd crossed the lane.

Once before, in the 11th grade,
She'd stood with roses, love displayed.
A letter, sweet words, a heart so true,
But he, with a burden, refused to pursue.

"I've got my dreams, and duties to bear,
A relationship now, I cannot share."
He said with a sigh, and walked away,
Not knowing what tomorrow would convey.

Years flew by, as time always does,
He saw her once more, with someone who was
By her side, so happy, love in full bloom,
And the boy smiled softly, no hint of gloom.

For he'd moved on, as life had its plan,
Now he had a wife, and kids in the span
Of days that had passed, so full of grace,
He'd forgotten the past, life found its place.

In his heart, no regrets, no more pain,
Just love and laughter, and dreams to sustain.
And he laughed at himself, so carefree and wise,
That sometimes, the heart knows no compromise.

For time heals all, and life moves on,
With love that grows and continues to dawn.
Now content, with a family so bright,
The boy had found his perfect light.

30. Aromatic Zeal

In the bright hum of the workplace, a spark ignites,
A rhythm of voices, a sea of delight.
But then, like a whisper, a fragrance so bold,
The aroma of biryani, a story untold.

Rich spices and warmth filled the very air,
A tempting allure, too perfect to spare.
Mouths began watering, eyes filled with glee,
A feast was unfolding, a moment to be.

Like an angel descending, with kindness in hand,
A friend brought the biryani, a gift so grand.
A fatherly figure, a brotherly guide,
Through moments of care, they'd always confide.

The rice was a symphony, the flavors divine,
Each bite a treasure, a taste so fine.
But it wasn't just food that warmed every soul,
It was wisdom in each grain, making hearts whole.

She thanked him with tears, for his love and grace,
A friend who had guided her through time and space.
A meal of such beauty, a gift beyond measure,
In biryani's warmth, she'd found life's true treasure.

31. Resonance

In the silence of creation, a spark took flight,
A canvas lay still, awaiting the light.
The brush in his hand, trembling with grace,
As memories of a girl filled the space.

The image of Shivaji, proud and divine,
Worshipping the God, his spirit aligned.
But as his hands moved with a trembling glow,
A flower bloomed where the paint did flow.

The melody of "Shiv Kailasi" in the air,
Goosebumps rose as though she were there.
Her essence, her presence, woven in time,
In every stroke, her soul did chime.

Flowers of wonder, a gift to the Lord,
Crafted by hands that were never bored.
Each petal, each leaf, a prayer to the sky,
A masterpiece born from a love that won't die.

In the magic of the moment, she stood by his side,
Tears in their eyes, as the truth couldn't hide.
She was the gem, the muse of his art,
The echo of her love, forever in his heart.

Together they wept, but joy filled their eyes,
For in her, he'd found the greatest of ties.
A creation, a bond, forever to stay—
A masterpiece born from love's pure display.

32. Fading Stars

She whispered of love, with promises so sweet,
A bond built on trust, two hearts in heartbeat.
Together they dreamed, of future so bright,
Their love was a flame, a beacon of light.

She prayed in temples, knelt in mosque's grace,
Each prayer whispered, seeking love's embrace.
Through rituals and vows, she sought her way,
Hoping that love would never stray.

But winds of change, a storm soon unfurled,
Her aunt's harsh voice, a disruption to her world.
With restrictions and force, the girl had no say,
She was bound by duty, in life's cruel play.

The boy, her love, shattered at the news,
His heart broke in silence, with nothing to lose.
His world turned dark, with no clear light,
As she walked toward a future that felt so trite.

One final night, on the mountain they stood,
In silence they wept, for the love that once could.
The stars faded softly, as tears fell like rain,
A love once eternal, now bound by pain.

They cried together, the moon their only friend,
For the love they had, had come to its end.
In each other's arms, they found their last peace,
As love faded gently, leaving only the cease.

33. Enduring

In the quiet of the canvas, strokes begin to fly,
A story told in colors, beneath the vast, bold sky.
Shivaji, lost in moments, his mind begins to race,
A bond with his gem, no time could erase.

The paintbrush quivers, a memory takes its place,
Of promises whispered, of love and grace.
He thought of the moments they'd shared in the past,
And how their connection would always last.

His heart felt a tremor, a warmth from within,
A love so profound, where words couldn't begin.
As he painted her image, his soul started to weep,
A promise to share, a secret to keep.

"Once I return," he thought with a vow,
"I'll tell her of this, of where I am now."
A bond so eternal, in silence they grieve,
For in each other's hearts, they both believe.

Her absence left him speechless, a tear in his eye,
Yet in that quiet sorrow, no words could defy.
For in that one thought, in that lingering prayer,
They were together—forever, beyond compare.

34. Whispers of the Infinite

In silence deep, where stars unfold,
The universe, a tale untold.
It whispers soft, a secret kept,
In every dream, where wishes slept.

A teacher wise, both pure and kind,
It shapes the heart, it clears the mind.
With quiet force, unseen, it moves,
The path we seek, the life we choose.

Desire's spark, a flame so bright,
Ignites the dark, becomes the light.
No need for words, just thoughts so clear,
The universe listens, always near.

Through winds that howl, through storms that rage,
It opens doors, it turns the page.
From chaos wild, to peace untold,
It guides us through, both young and old.

The secrets held in nature's chest,
Are pathways carved for hearts to rest.
In quiet trust, I found my way,
And peace arrived, at break of day.

A silent wish, a powerful thought,
The universe grants, the answers sought.
Its mystery deep, its wisdom vast,
A force to guide, to hold, to last.

35. The Gift Of A Lifetime

A decade passed, like shadows long,
Time weaving silence, life moved along.
Then came a day, rare as the moon,
A gift awaited, a heart in tune.

A ring of stones, with rubies bright,
And emeralds gleaming, soft with light.
Each gem a spark, each stone a star,
A treasure of beauty, near and far.

He called her "gem," with gentle grace,
As if the heavens had touched his face.
He shyly stepped, withdrew, then waited,
His heart was full, his soul elated.

She saw him glance, her eyes met his,
And in that moment, pure joy was his.
A gift of love, wrapped in shy delight,
A symbol to hold, shining so bright.

Her heart leaped high, her spirits soared,
This was the gift she had once adored.
She kissed the ring, her smile so wide,
Her joy flowed out, she could not hide.

A special moment, rare and true,
A token of love, the heart's breakthrough.
She kept it close, within her heart,
A bond unbroken, never to part.

Though the giving was quiet, slow,
The love behind it was all aglow.
For in that gem, a promise shone—
A gift of a lifetime, forever her own.

36. Unbound

She walks in silence, but her heart is loud,
A girl in a world that's forever bowed.
The walls they build, the chains they cast,
She wears them all, but not to last.

Beneath the weight of years untold,
Her dreams are forged, her spirit bold.
The rules of old, the words they say,
She'll tear them down, come break of day.

In the corners where they try to hide,
She finds the fire they can't divide.
Her voice is rising, wild and free,
She'll carve her path, and let it be.

She is the storm, the sun, the sky,
Not bound by limits, not born to comply.
With every step, she shatters glass,
A revolution in the making—she'll surpass.

She dreams of a world where she can stand,
Not by their rules, but by her hand.
No cage can hold what longs to soar,
She is unbound—forevermore.

37. A Final Wish Before Goodbye

In the silence of the night, he hears her name,
A whisper soft, yet it burns like flame.
Though miles and time stand in between,
Her voice is the thread that keeps them unseen.

They never touched, never shared a kiss,
Yet their souls knew a love, pure and blissed.
They spoke through words that traveled far,
The distance just a shadow, their hearts the star.

He has built a life, and she built hers too,
But still, he wonders if she feels this too—
A longing, a pull, that never fades,
A love that time and space forbade.

He dreams of meeting her, just once more,
To see her eyes, feel what they adore.
Before the world steals them away,
Before his heart can no longer stay.

They've never been bound by touch or skin,
But their connection runs deep, from within.
Her voice, a balm to his restless soul,
A bond so strong, it makes him whole.

Though they've been denied by fate's cruel hand,
He knows she understand, she'll always stand,
Beside him, in spirit, in thought, in dream,
They are the echoes of a love that gleams.

So, before he goes, just one more time,
Let him hear her voice, let their hearts chime.
For though their love may never see the light,
It lives within them, forever bright.

38. Echoes of a Forgotten Promise

She stirs in the quiet of her busy days,
Among laughter and toys, in the soft, loving haze.
Her husband's arms, her children's cheer,
But in the stillness, a whisper draws near.

A fleeting thought, a shadow from the past,
Of promises made, too beautiful to last.
They'd spoken of forever, of dreams to unfold,
A love so fierce, so bright, so bold.

But time, with its cruel, unyielding hands,
Wove a different fate, built upon shifting sands.
She wears the role, the wife, the mother true,
Yet inside, a secret, a love she once knew.

Her heart, now torn, struggles to keep
A promise buried too deep to speak.
Her mind wanders back to the nights of youth,
When their love was a fire, raw and uncouth.

She aches in silence, her soul feeling frail,
Caught between love that must prevail
And the years she's built, the life she's made,
A beautiful home, where memories fade.

Her heart still longs for what could have been,
For a love that's lost in the space between.
Restless, she wonders if he feels it too—
The love they promised, forever true.

But now, with the years that swiftly fly,
She smiles through the ache, and holds back a sigh.
Her children, her love, her life—her song,
But inside, her heart beats for a love long gone.

39. Bound by her Endless Love

In the stillness where our mother once stood,
Her love, now a memory, as soft as the wood.
The days feel heavy, the nights cold and long,
But, my brothers, together, we'll stay strong.

Though she's gone, her spirit remains,
In every tear, in every pain.
The strength she gave us, we hold it tight,
Guiding us through the darkest night.

I promise, my brothers, through all the years,
To stand beside you, to calm your fears.
When the world feels too big, and hearts too small,
I'll be the bridge, we won't fall.

In her absence, we are not alone,
For in each other, love has grown.
We'll carry her wisdom, her warmth, her grace,
And find her love in every embrace.

So let us grieve, let us heal,
But let our bond be our shield.
As her children, we'll rise above,
Bound together by her endless love.

40. Wrapped in Silence

She wears her smile like a silent plea,
A mask for the love he fails to see.
His gifts are wrapped in ribbons bright,
But they miss the heart, the soul's true light.

Diamonds, pearls, and silken thread,
Things she cannot wear in her head.
His gestures grand, though kind in thought,
But still, they leave her heart distraught.

For in his eyes, she's just a prize,
Not someone with dreams or silent cries.
He offers trinkets, jewels, and gold,
But never hears the stories she's never told.

Each gift, a token to ease his guilt,
But it can't replace the love she's built.
In quiet moments, when the night is still,
She longs for him to feel, to hear, to will.

A simple touch, a whispered word,
To know the silence that goes unheard.
But he, wrapped in his ignorance, stays
And she, in the quiet, fades away.

41. Wings Unfurling

I dream of skies so extensive, so free,
Where I can rise, just me, just me.
But here I stand, with strings unseen,
Enslaved in a place that isn't serene.

You're by my side, yet worlds apart,
I reach for you, but miss your heart.
In stillness, I weep, in shade I stay,
Yearning for words you won't say.

I celebrate in joy, yet you don't see,
My heart beats loud, but it's lost in the breeze.
In my chuckle, there's sorrow untold,
A story of loneliness, quietly bold.

I wanted love, not this void space,
Not to be lost in a cold embrace.
You're there, yet I perceive so far,
Like a fantasy I once held, now a sinking star.

I want to run, to fly, to break,
To abandon behind this heartache.
I desire someone who will hear my voice,
Someone who cognizes that I have a choice.

I extend for liberty, for someone to see,
The girl within who longs to be free.
In a world unleashed, I'll finally stand,
With wings outstretched, unfurling new land

42. The Unbreakable Trio

From childhood days so bright and free,
Three friends stood strong—just meant to be.
Neil, Rhutu, and Khushi's bond so tight,
A friendship glowing, warm with light.

Different souls yet hearts as one,
Their journey together was full of fun.
One a dancer, with grace so true,
One for defense, in passion she grew.
One loved the fields, in sports he shined,
Each with a dream, a path designed.

Festivals came, and they'd unite,
Lamps would glow and hearts felt light.
Vacations spent with laughter sweet,
An outing planned—oh, what a treat!

Jokes and pranks in endless spree,
A bond so strong, wild and free.

People watched with pure delight,
Saying, "This is friendship right!"

But time soon called them far and wide,
Each a journey to decide.
Adolescence came with paths apart,
Yet distance never stole their heart.

Though life took turns in varied ways,
Still in sorrow, still in praise,
They stood beside with love so grand,
Three friends, forever, hand in hand.

A friendship meant to last the years,
Through smiles, through trials, even tears.
For though their roads may twist and bend,
They are, and will be—friends till the end!

43. The Hoodie Boy Who Taught Me to Laugh

He walked in with a quiet charm,
A hoodie draped, no trace of harm.
A football player, fierce on the field,
Yet in his smile, a warmth was revealed.

He wasn't just known for his game,
But for a heart that never sought fame.
With every laugh, with every glance,
He gave a friendship, a second chance.

He taught me how to cherish the day,
To find the joy in work and play.
In moments heavy, when life felt tight,
He showed me how to embrace the light.

His smile, a beacon in the crowd,

A gem of a person, humble and proud.
A lesson in laughter, in kindness and cheer,
He wiped away sorrow, replaced it with clear.

Famous not just for his skill or name,
But for a spirit that couldn't be tamed.
The hoodie boy, a legend, so true,
Gave me a friendship, and a world anew.

Though the world may know him for his game,
To me, he's a teacher, never seeking fame.
A friend who taught me, in every way,
To laugh, to cherish, and brighten my day.

44. Magnificent Titans

Lost is the heart amidst somewhere,
Puzzled with the way how to reach there.

The dazzling glare endeavor to reach the darkness,
Striving invariably to flourish a harness.

Straddling in the ocean anticipating an assist,
Dissembling in the obscurity, read to hold the fist.

It seems they run and run but fail to find the way,
The journey continues with rush and gush where lay.

Discern the radiant in the isle,
There sits the heart scared and thinking all the while.

People seek to reach but impede their mind,
Adolescents they say has made them blind.

Guru is the light to touch the soul,
It is the eternal truth, who helps to find the goal.

Leave your worries bring trust ahead,
This beacon of showers will surely rethread.

Guru Shishya bond is imperishable,
For you to preserve is favourable.

Connection is set up and light brightens,
Found the heart with Magnificent Titans.

45. What do you mean by Freedom?

What do you mean by freedom?
For a few thrill and for others boredom.
Struggle for existence prevail everywhere,
The gates of paradise are found nowhere.

Is this the India,
envisioned by our leaders,
Are we giving justice to their sacrifices,
or making the life more tougher.

Today's youth is lost in hatred and dark,
Its our virtuous obligation to brighten their path.
In this fast world, they need a companion,
To cherish, to rejoice, to rejuvenate their union.

Still there are boundaries, religion, misfortune,
Still it is a world of imposed curfew
where people do not allow others to live
and also to live through.

What do you mean by freedom?
For few virtue, for few loss,
Struggle for existence prevails everywhere.
Life is a big toss.

Acceptance and Realization are necessary,
For teens, for youths, for kids, for old,
Freedom is meant for all.
But still there's life that take folds,
Always has something that holds.

What do you mean by freedom?
What do you mean by freedom?

46. Her Voice, Her Fight

They speak of equality, loud and proud,
Yet silence falls where truth is found.
If men and women walk as one,
Then why is justice left undone?

A morning dawned, a thought took flight,
A conversation bathed in light.
I spoke of women, bold and free,
But chains of fate he showed to me.

"A woman's world is home and hearth,
Not business plans, not dreams of worth.
She serves, she cooks, she bends, she stays
Her destiny in duty lays."

Oh, tell me, where is justice now?
Why must she kneel, why must she bow?
A daughter leaves her home behind,
Yet as a stranger, she's confined.

She gives her love, her care, her trust,
Yet still, she bears the weight of "must."
Respect them all, yet be denied,
Adjust, obey—her fate is tied.

She earns, she toils, yet bears the load,
A silent strength, a path untold.
Her parents—guests at their own child's door,
Giving, giving—forevermore.

I ask the world, what do you see?
What is this "equality"?
Malala rose, unchained, unbowed,
Kiran stood tall, both fierce and proud.
Draupadi's voice shook halls of power,
Priyanka shone, her finest hour.

Yet still, the world turns cold and blind,
To those left struggling far behind.
A woman carries life anew,
Yet who will carry her pain through?

Hear her cries, her silent screams,
The burdened heart, the shattered dreams.
Change begins where thoughts transform,
Where justice breaks the ancient norm.

Respect her, lift her, let her fly,
No longer caged beneath the sky.
For only when she stands as free,
Will rise a world of true equality.

47. An Incomplete Journey

You've gone, yet still I feel you near,
In every corner, every tear.
Your smile, your mischief, your teasing ways,
Are echoes of our brighter days.

You were the heartbeat, the soul of our home,
Now I stand here, so lost, so alone.
The laughter, the chaos, the warmth you brought,
Now silent, a void that can't be bought.

You left behind so many tasks,
Responsibilities, no one asks.
How do I carry this weight alone?
How do I make our house a home?

The care for Dad, your gentle touch,
Your bond with him, I miss so much.
Your love for my brothers, your playful jest,
I fear I can't fill those roles — I try my best.

And little ones, my sweet little boys,
I'm lost, Mama, in this swirling world.
How do I comfort them, make them smile,
When I'm unsure of walking this mile?

You knew how to hold it all together,
With grace, with love, in every weather.
Your mischief and laughter, a joy so bright,
You'd ease all our worries with your light.

But now, it's me, and I'm unsure,
How to handle all this, how to endure.
I'll carry your legacy, your love so true,
But Mama, how do I do this without you?

I'll try to smile, to stand tall and strong,
To care for them all, to right what's wrong.
But the truth is, I need you still,
To guide me through, to help me heal.

Your laughter, your mischief, your love so wide,
I'll keep them close, deep inside.
And with each step, I'll remember you,
How you loved us all, and saw us through.

48. Legacy

As the years have passed, I've watched you grow,
From shy beginnings to the confidence you now show.
Each day with you, a gift, a treasure untold,
In your laughter and kindness, my heart takes hold.

Through all the lessons, both hard and sweet,
You've stood by me, making this journey complete.
The days we've shared, the smiles, the tears,
Are memories I'll cherish throughout the years.

Your gestures of love, so pure and sincere,
A birthday wish that brought me near a tear.
A Teachers' Day, so thoughtful, full of grace,
Made every moment with you shine in this space.

Your gratitude, like a warm embrace,
Has filled my soul, put a smile on my face.
The small acts, the hugs, the words so kind,
Are treasures that I'll carry in my mind.

In each of you, I see a bright star,
Shining so brightly, no matter how far.
The world awaits you, full of dreams to pursue,
But know, in my heart, I'll always be with you.

So here's my thanks, from the depths of my heart,
For the joy, the love, the way you all play your part.
May you continue to grow, to love, and to dream,
For you are the light of this teacher's life, it seems.

Thank you, my dear ones, for all that you've done,
The journey with you has just begun.
With gratitude and love, I send you today,
A wish for success, in every way.

49. The Dilemma of Leaving

In the midst of the winters,
there came the news.
The invigilators for the Boards,
in VIBGYOR filled with the hues...

The tantrums, the traffic, the strange visages,
With cold welcome and shattering glasses,
Trolled on the way with edu-collaboration,
With a promise to part the responsibility to serve the
nation.

A new enterprise, a roller-coaster ride,
Riding everyday to manage inner tide,
As the day passed the bonding increase,
But people seek opportunity to get it cease.

The courage, the valor every person shows,
All the obstacles, all the strolls, the shaking hospitality,
Were taken care in an optimistic way by various rows,
dine, laugh, merry and chat, a unique world build with

serenity.

The moment has come to move apart,
With all joys and sorrows filled in our heart.
With the promise to remember and keep caring,
Unbearable, the dilemma of leaving.

50. Grandma's Love

The kitchen still smells of namkin parathas,
Where her hands once danced, soft as a breeze,
Her laughter, a melody I can't forget,
And the way she'd call me, "Beta," with ease.

Her touch, her affection, a bond so true,
We were best friends, not just me and you.
In every moment, you'd stand by my side,
When the world was against me, you were my guide.

I'll never forget that November night,
When you left, and everything turned to night.
I missed you, Grandma, more than words can tell,
I wasn't there, I blame myself.

At the funeral, your spirit filled the air,
In the corners, your footsteps echoed everywhere.
No one to talk to, just silence, just pain,
The house felt empty, nothing felt the same.

But now, I'm walking the path you dreamt,
Every success is a promise I've kept.
I carry your love, your lessons, your grace,
And I'll make you proud, in every place.

Though you're not here, your strength remains,
In my heart, your love still sustains.
I'll rise, I'll conquer, as you always believed,
Grandma, for you, I will achieve.

51. New Poem

* 9 7 8 9 3 6 9 5 3 4 7 5 3 *